PuzzleMania
Puzzles for Beginners

HIGHLIGHTS PRESS

Honesdale, Pennsylvania

Contents

When you finish a puzzle, check it off √. Good luck, and happy puzzling!

Galaxy Quest

Each of these spaceships has something in common with the other two spaceships in the same row. For example, in the first row across all three spaceships have antennae on top. Look at the other rows across, down, and diagonally. Can you tell what's alike in each row?

ILLUSTRATION BY JIM PAILLOT

Beach Find

The names of 18 beach things are hidden in the letters. Some words are across. Others are up and down. We found SHOVEL. Can you find the rest?

Word List

BALL
BREEZE
CHAIR
FLIP-FLOPS
HAT
OCEAN
PAIL
SAND
SEA GULL
SEAWEED
SHELL
~~SHOVEL~~
STARFISH
SUN
SWIMSUIT
TOWEL
TREE
WAVE

```
K O C E A N B A L L
X J K S H E L L F H
J Q S E A G U L L A
Y X S W I M S U I T
T O W E L S H S P B
R Y A C J U O A F R
E Q V H X N V N L E
E S E A W E E D O E
Y P A I L X L K P Z
S T A R F I S H S E
```

Shell Game

Can you find the two seashells that are the same?

ILLUSTRATION BY CLAY CANTRELL

7

Rhino Route

START

Can you help this rhinoceros get to the water hole? Find a clear path from START to FINISH.

FINISH

Double Pets

Which pet would you choose? The two pet-shop pictures are the same but different. Point out what's missing on this page.

Wiggle Snacks

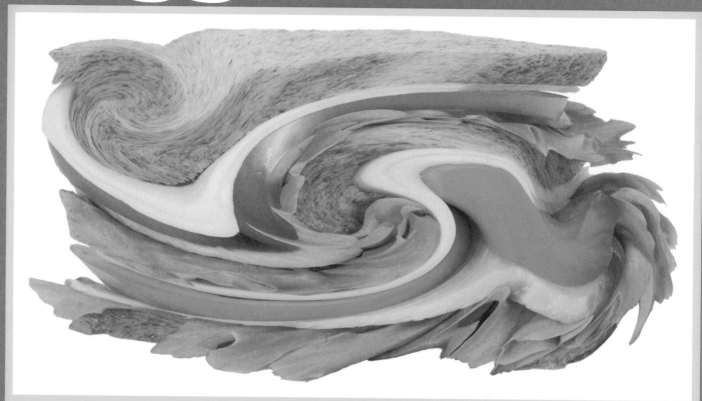

These foods look like they have taken a turn in the blender. Can you guess what each one is?

Play It

ILLUSTRATION BY RON ZALME

Fill-in Fun
Color each space that has a dot to see a surprise.

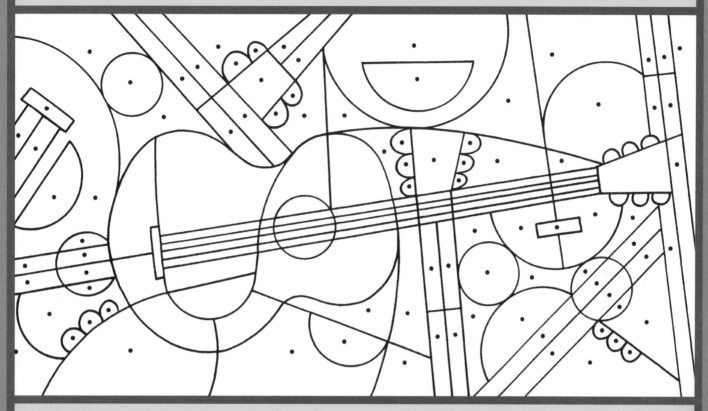

Color Copy
Use markers or crayons to make a matching piñata.

13

Caps Search

Go, team, go! There are lots of caps at the ball game.
Can you find all 11?

Can you
find?
Can you also find
five hot dogs in the
picture?

ILLUSTRATION BY DONNA CATANESE

15

At the Movies

Can you find these 12 Hidden Pictures® in the theater lobby?

eyeglasses

firefighter's hat

pencil

butterfly

key

slice of watermelon

sheep

log

fish

pumpkin

flower

shovel

What's Playing?

Connect the dots from 1 to 26 to see what the movie is today.

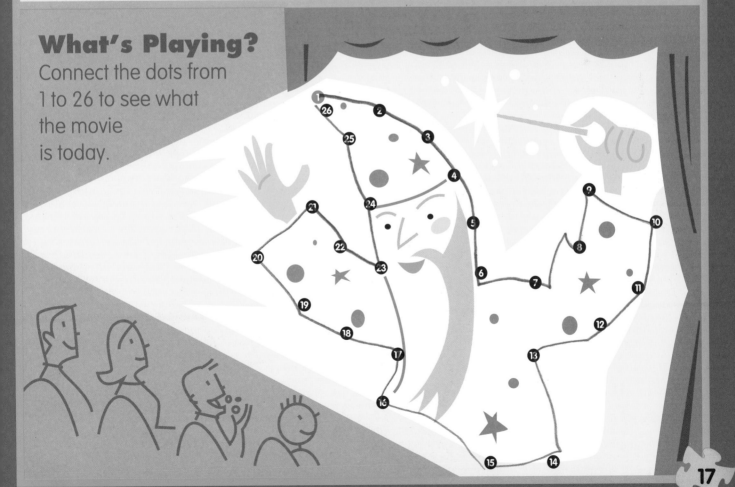

17

Critter Five

1. Name three words that rhyme with **tug**.

2. Can you name three animals with horns or antlers?

3. Circle the animal with the most spots.

4. The giraffe is the world's tallest animal.
○ True ○ False

5. Giant pandas come from what country?
○ Kenya ○ China ○ Brazil

Treat Trail

Help this hamster find the one path that will lead him to his treats.

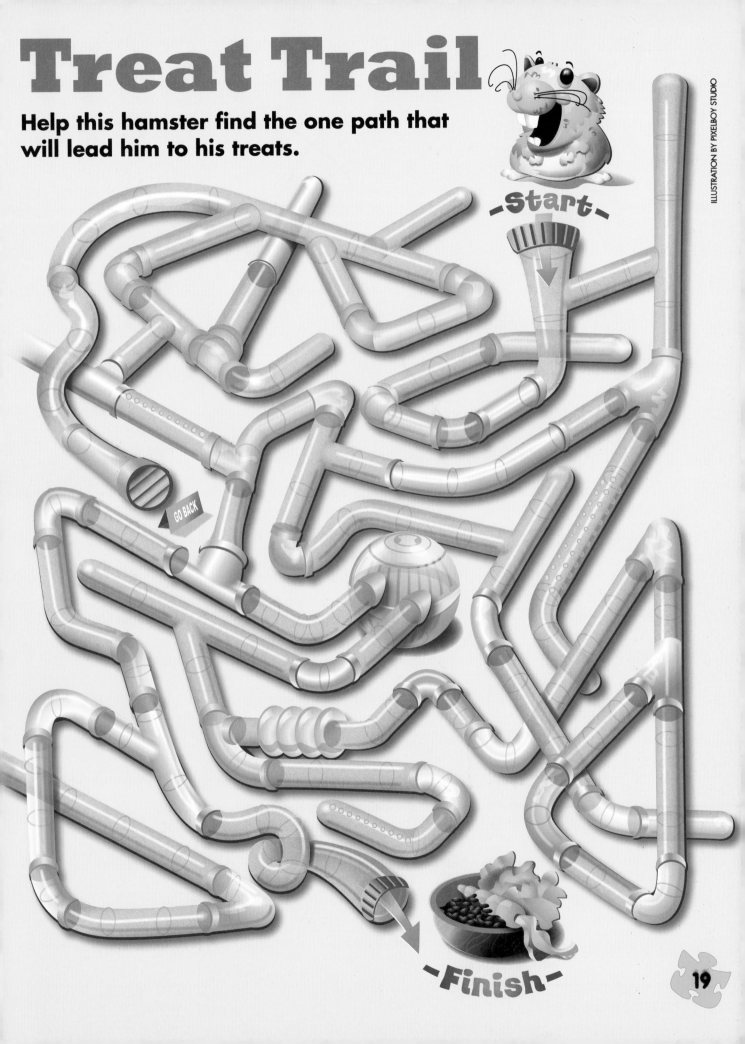

-Start-

GO BACK

-Finish-

19

ILLUSTRATION BY PIXELBOY STUDIO

Balloon Match

Every hot-air balloon in the picture has one that looks just like it. Find all 10 matching pairs.

ILLUSTRATION BY DAVE JOLY

Frog Code

There are jokes about frogs on the next page. Use the frog code to fill in the letters and finish the jokes. Then tell them to your friends!

A

C

D

E

H

I

K

L

N

O

P

R

S

T

Y

What is a frog's favorite drink?

C R O A K - A - C O L A

What did the bus driver say to the frog?

" H O P   O N !"

Where do frogs make notes?

O N   L I L Y   P A D S

What do frogs wear on their feet?

O P E N - T O E D

S H O E S

Boat Find

The names of 16 ways to get around on the water are hidden in the letters. Some words are across. Others are up and down. We found SHIP. Can you find the rest?

Word List

- BARGE
- CANOE
- CLIPPER
- FERRY
- HOUSEBOAT
- JET SKI
- KAYAK
- LIFEBOAT
- MOTORBOAT
- RAFT
- ROWBOAT
- SAILBOAT
- SHIP
- TANKER
- TUGBOAT
- YACHT

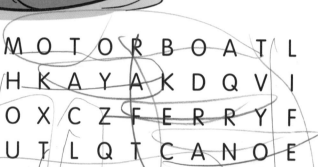

```
M O T O R B O A T L
H K A Y A K D Q V I
O X C Z F E R R Y F
U T L Q T C A N O E
S A I L B O A T S B
E N P B A R G E H O
B K P J E T S K I A
O E E Y A C H T P T
A R R O W B O A T D
T U G B O A T V D Z
```

24

Parrot Pals

Can you find the two parrots that are the same?

25

Funny Flights

The Smith kids are trying out their new paper airplane designs. Follow the paths to find out where each one's plane landed.

ILLUSTRATION BY DAVID COULSON

LEMONADE

S Is For ?

Can you find a seal, a sandwich, and a sunflower? What other things can you find that begin with the letter S?

ILLUSTRATION BY DAVE KLUG

Tongue Twister
Try to say this three times as fast as you can: **Selfish shellfish.**

Wiggle Insects

**These insects go this way and that.
Can you guess what each one is?**

Color It

Fill-in Fun Color each space that has a dot to make a big animal.

Color by Number Color the peacock with markers or crayons.

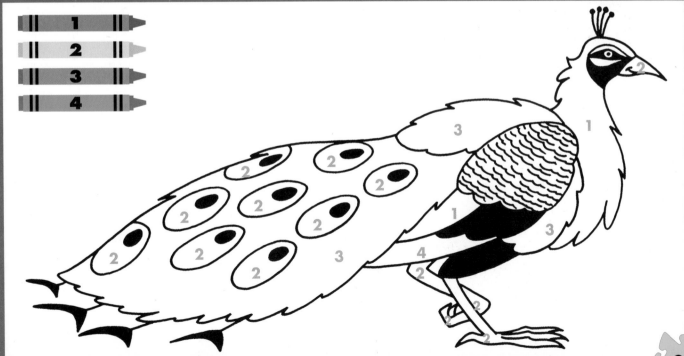

Touchdown!

START

Help Ned score a touchdown. Find a path from START to FINISH. If you come to a person, choose a different path.

FINISH

Double Desert

That is one tall cactus! These scenic pictures are the same but different. What's missing on this page?

Name Five

1. What instrument is this girl playing?
○ flute ◉ trombone ○ tuba

2. The Spanish word "hermano" means brother.
◉ True ○ False

3. What are three girls' names that begin with the letter C?

4. Name four animals you find in the water.

5. Which planet is the largest in our solar system?
○ Saturn ◉ Jupiter ○ Earth

Pie Way

Patti just pulled her pie from the oven. Can you help her get it to the bake-off before it cools?

Start

Finish

ILLUSTRATION BY MIKE MORAN

44

3

7

1

Judge

37

Bow Search

This dog show has plenty of bows!
Can you find 20 in the picture?

Can you find?
Two of the dogs look the same. Can you find them?

BEST IN SHOW

ILLUSTRATION BY SCOTT BURROUGHS

In the Kitchen

ILLUSTRATION BY DAVE KLUG

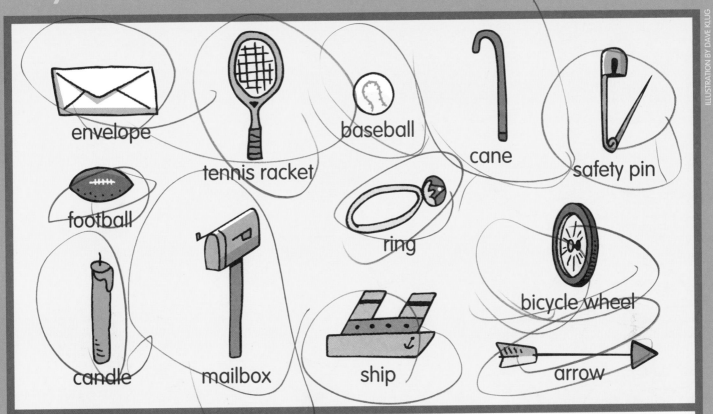

envelope

tennis racket

baseball

cane

safety pin

football

ring

bicycle wheel

candle

mailbox

ship

arrow

What's for Dinner?

Connect the dots from 1 to 24 to make today's special.

41

Tree Find

The names of 18 trees are hidden in the letters. Some words are across. Others are up and down. We found PEAR. Can you find the rest?

Word List

- ASH
- ASPEN
- BEECH
- BIRCH
- CEDAR
- CHESTNUT
- DOGWOOD
- ELM
- FIR
- MAPLE
- OAK
- PALM
- PEAR
- PINE
- REDWOOD
- SPRUCE
- WALNUT
- WILLOW

```
J A S P E N O W Q
V F P A L M A A X
B I R C H Y K L R
E R U Z J P I N E
E Y C E D A R U D
C H E S T N U T W
H Q L V P E A R O
X Z M A P L E Y O
Y J D O G W O O D
W I L L O W A S H
```

42

Caterpillar Pair

ILLUSTRATION BY CLAY CANTRELL

Flag Match

Every flapping pennant in the picture has one that looks just like it. Find all 10 matching pairs.

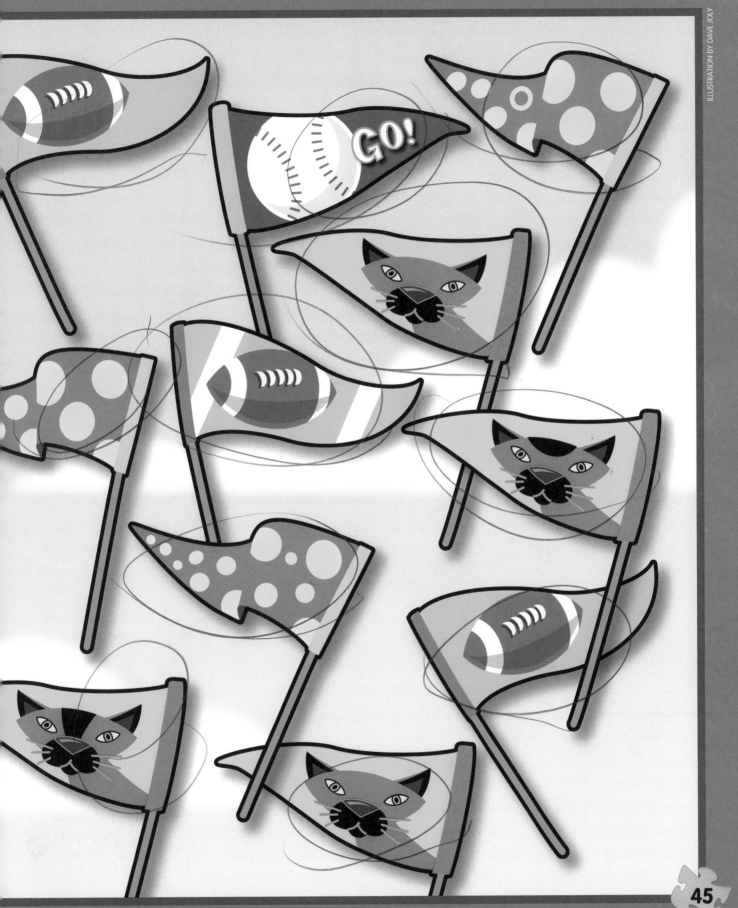

ILLUSTRATION BY DAVE JOLY

Dinosaur Code

There are jokes about dinosaurs on the next page. Use the dinosaur code to fill in the letters and finish the jokes. Then tell them to your friends!

What do you call a sleeping dinosaur?

A S T E G O -
S h o r E - u s

What do you call a worried dinosaur?

N E R V O U S R E X

What does a triceratops sit on?

I T S T O I C E R A -
B T O M

Wiggle Wheels

These vehicles are speeding by in a blur. Can you guess what each one is?

Ride It

Fill-in Fun Color each space that has a dot to make a picture.

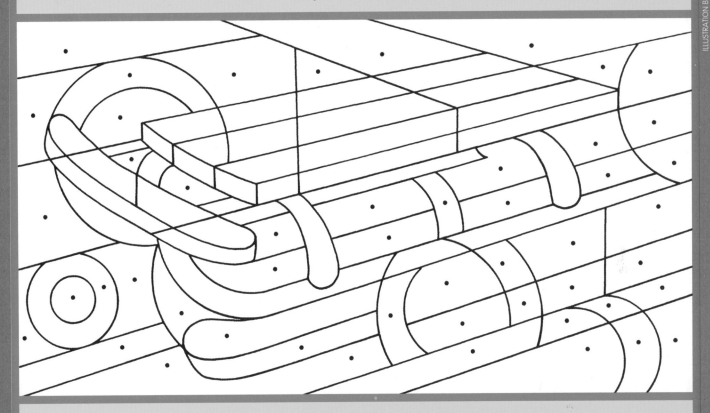

Color Copy Use markers or crayons to make a matching train.

Cat Course

WHISKERS

ZIPPY

TOM

These kitties have places to go! Follow their paths to see where each is heading.

51

Count On It!

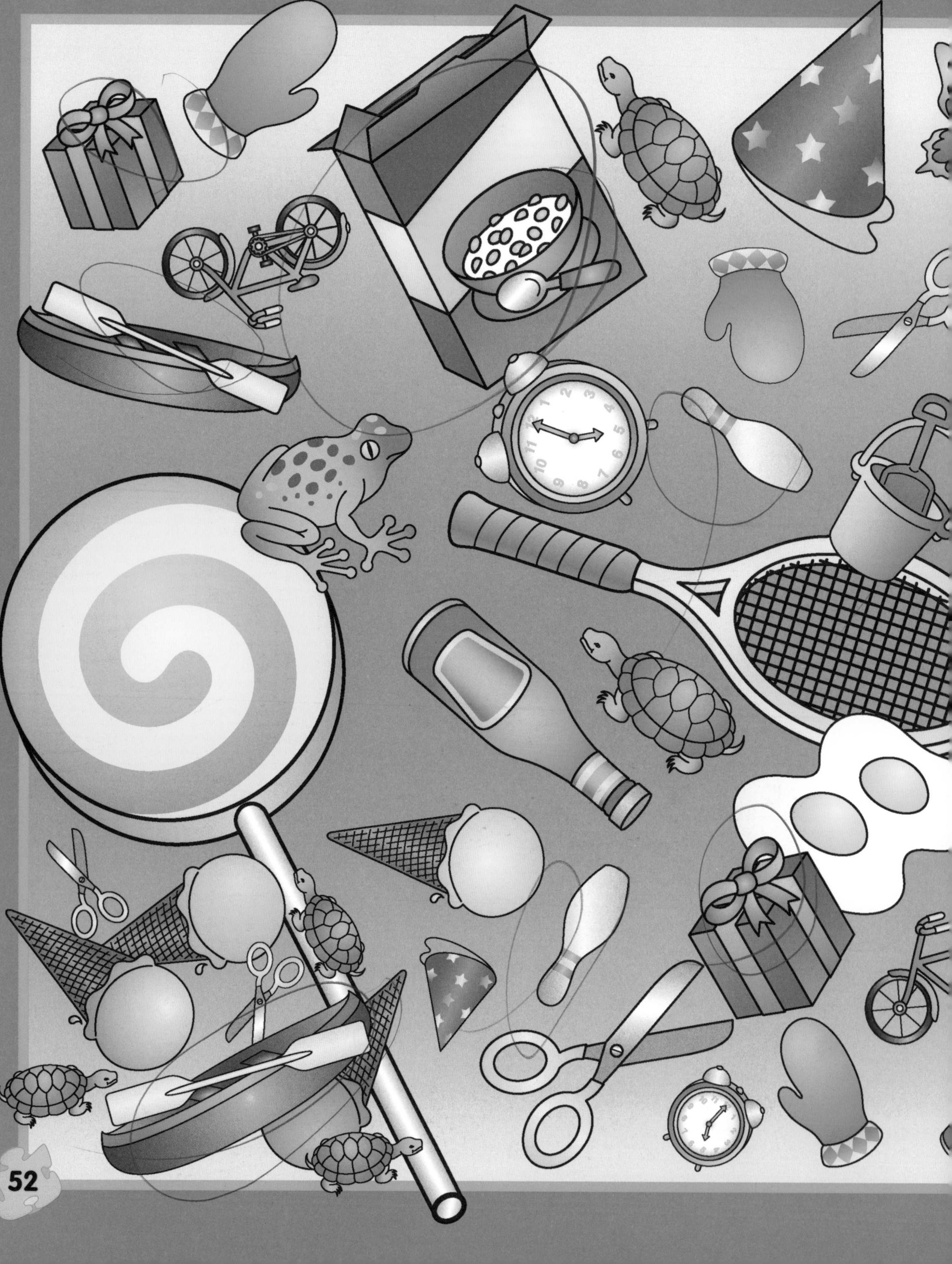

ILLUSTRATION BY RITA LASCARO

Lunch Find

The names of 17 lunch-box favorites are hidden in the letters. Some words are across. Others are up and down. We found YOGURT. Can you find the rest?

ILLUSTRATION BY JACK DESROCHER

Word List

APPLE
BANANA
BREAD
CELERY
CHEESE
COOKIE
CRACKERS
GRAPES
JUICE
MILK
PEACH
RAISINS
SOUP
TACO CHIPS
TUNA FISH
TURKEY
YOGURT

```
C T A C O C H I P S
R V W E T U R K E Y
A P P L E J U I C E
C B R E A D M I L K
K A G R A P E S W P
E N X Y O G U R T E
R A I S I N S Z V A
S N C O O K I E E C
W A T U N A F I S H
S O U P C H E E S E
```

54

Swim Twins

Can you find the two fishbowls that are the same?

ILLUSTRATION BY CLAY CANTRELL

Roll With It!

START

Find a path for this roller-coaster car that does not pass another car. Follow the path from START to FINISH. Hold on tight!

FINISH

57

Double Serve

It is a perfect day for beach volleyball! These pictures are the same but different. What's missing on this page?

Field Wiggles

These animals are at home in forests, fields, and your backyard. Can you guess what each one is?

Wing It

ILLUSTRATION BY RON ZALME

Fill-in Fun
Color each space that has a dot to make a high flyer.

Color Copy
Use markers or crayons to color this butterfly.

Ball Search

There are lots of basketballs at this practice.
Can you find all 15?

Can you
find?

Can you also find
five pairs of red
sneakers?

ILLUSTRATION BY SCOTT BURROUGHS

63

Zoo Stars

Can you find these 12 Hidden Pictures® at the panda habitat?

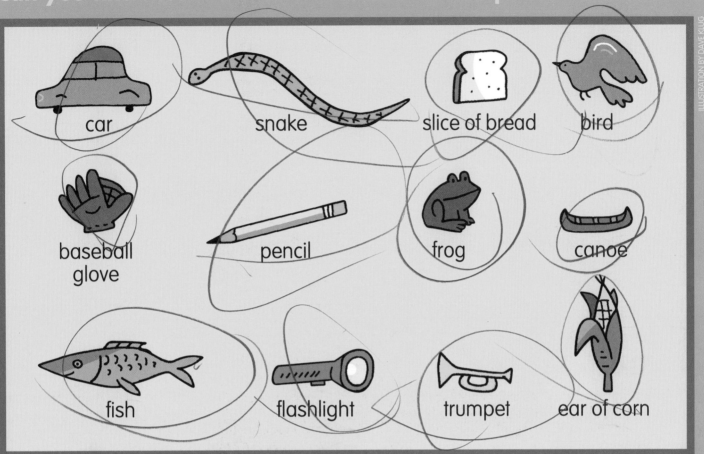

car

snake

slice of bread

bird

baseball glove

pencil

frog

canoe

fish

flashlight

trumpet

ear of corn

ILLUSTRATION BY DAVE KLUG

Who's at the Zoo?

Connect the dots from 1 to 32 to
see another zoo animal.

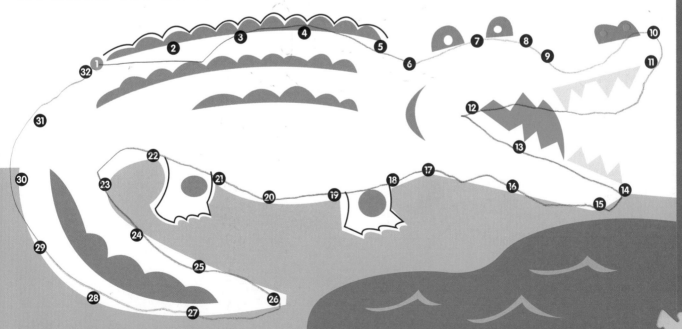

Travel Find

There are 18 ways to get around hidden in the letters. Some words are across. Others are up and down. We found TUGBOAT. Can you find the rest?

Word List

BIKE
CANOE
CAR
KAYAK
MOTORCYCLE
PLANE
ROWBOAT
SAILBOAT
SCOOTER
SHIP
SUBWAY
TAXI
TRACTOR
TRAIN
TRUCK
TUGBOAT
VAN
WAGON

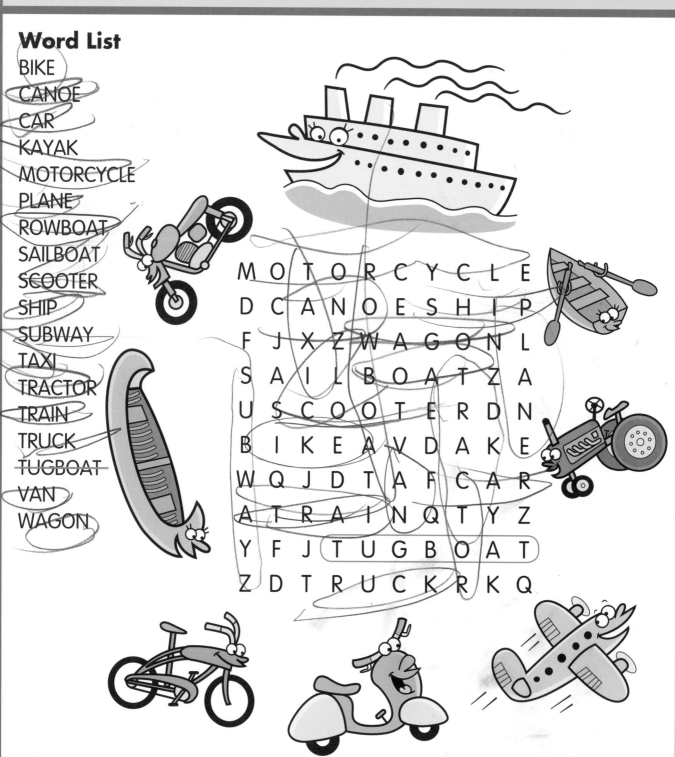

```
M O T O R C Y C L E
D C A N O E S H I P
F J X Z W A G O N L
S A I L B O A T Z A
U S C O O T E R D N
B I K E A V D A K E
W Q J D T A F C A R
A T R A I N Q T Y Z
Y F J T U G B O A T
Z D T R U C K R K Q
```

Moon Landing

Can you find the two spaceships that are the same?

Bunny Match

Every rabbit in the picture has one that looks just like it. Find all 10 matching pairs.

ILLUSTRATION BY DAVE JOLY

Fruit Code

There are jokes about fruit on the next page. Use the fruit code to fill in the letters and finish the jokes. Then tell them to your friends!

A

B

E

F

I

L

N

O

P

R

S

T

U

Y

What do you call an apple that plays the trumpet?

I T O O T I   F R U I T Y

What is a ghost's favorite fruit?

B O   O - B E R R I   E S

What do you call a cat that eats lemons?

A S O U R P U S S

What are two banana peels on the floor?

O N E   P A I R   O F
S L I P P E R S

Wiggle Gear

This outdoor gear is a bit shaky. Can you guess what each item is?

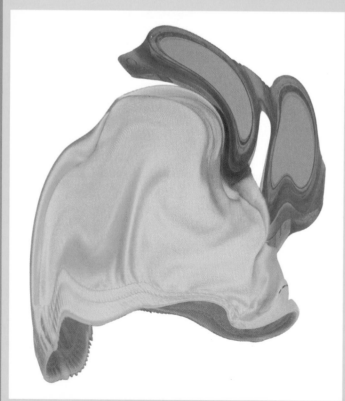

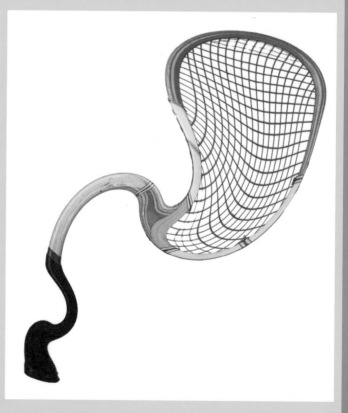

Wild Things

Fill-in Fun Color each space that has a dot to see a big animal.

Color by Number Color this dragonfly.

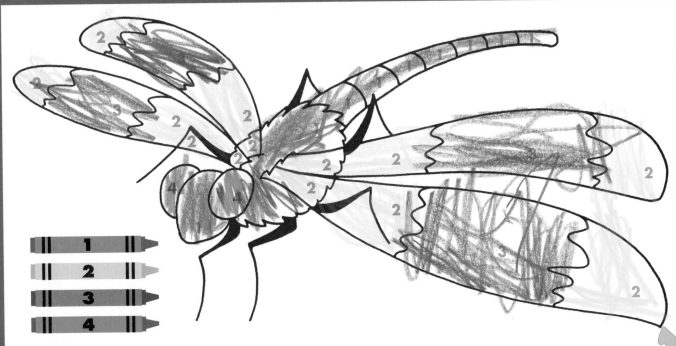

73

Leash Twist

The leashes at the dog park are twisted and tangled.
Follow each leash to match the owners with their pets.

A Is For ?

Can you find an astronaut, an ambulance, and an ant? What other things can you find that begin with the letter A?

ILLUSTRATION BY DAVE KLUG

Tongue Twister

Try to say this three times as fast as you can:

Amy ate almonds after Alfred.

Soccer Find

There are 18 soccer words hidden in the letters. Some words are across. Others are up and down. We found FOUL. Can you find the rest?

Word List

BALL
CLEATS
DEFENSE
DRIBBLE
FIELD
FOUL
GOALIE
HEADER
KICK
LOB
NET
OFFENSE
PERIOD
PASS
SAVE
SCORE
SHOT
SIDELINE

```
C L E A T S M P Q F
W L Z Y Y I D E J I
X O H E A D E R P E
M B A L L E F I A L
D R I B B L E O S D
K I C K Y I N D S S
Q O F F E N S E X H
M S C O R E E Z J O
X J Q U W Z Y N E T
G O A L I E S A V E
```

Bug Buddies

Can you find the two ladybug groups that are the same?

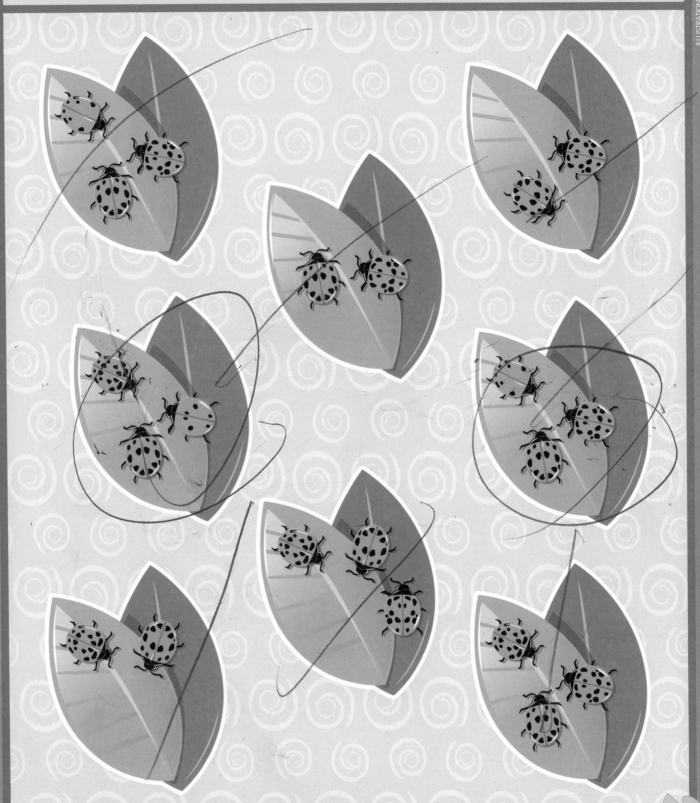

ILLUSTRATION BY CLAY CANTRELL

In the Deep

START

Help this diver find the treasure. Find a path from START to FINISH. Watch out for sea creatures that block your way!

FINISH

Double Builders

Mia and her dad are making a bookcase. These pictures are the same but different. What's missing on this page?

83

Wiggle Babies

These animal babies are a little wobbly. Can you guess what each one is?

84

Nothing to It!

Nineteen words or phrases that mean "nothing" are hidden up, down, across, backward, and diagonally. Find them all!

N V E U B
O V A C A N T
N O T H I N G J G
E C O M I S S I O N L L
P R K N Z E R O
N N E N Z N H T
N A D A I H P A L O V E
A I N P I L Z O E D
D N C I B I I M P
A B M C L L S I P U
B V O I D S C S T
W T U O T U H S H T Y
X G G E E S O O G
I N A U G H T
N U L L Q

Word List

- ~~BLANK~~
- ~~CIPHER~~
- ~~EMPTY~~
- ~~GOOSE EGG~~
- ~~LOVE~~
- ~~NADA~~
- NAUGHT
- ~~NIL~~
- ~~NIX~~
- ~~NONE~~
- ~~NOTHING~~
- ~~NULL~~
- ~~OMISSION~~
- ~~SHUT OUT~~
- ~~VACANT~~
- ~~VOID~~
- ~~ZERO~~
- ~~ZILCH~~
- ~~ZIP~~

Flag Search

There are lots of flags on this busy block. Can you find all 11?

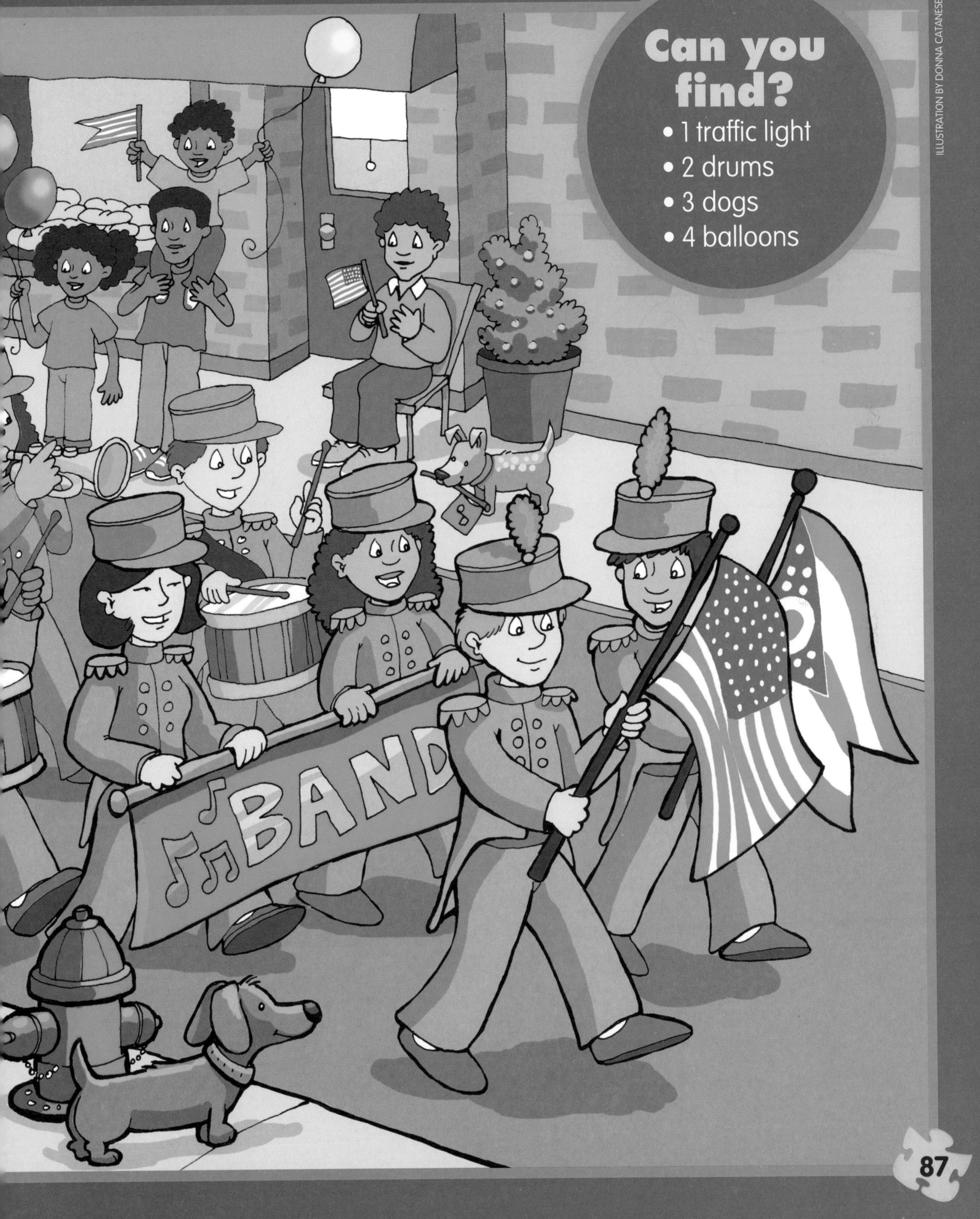

Can you find?

- 1 traffic light
- 2 drums
- 3 dogs
- 4 balloons

BAND

Bird Watchers

Can you find these 12 Hidden Pictures® among the birds?

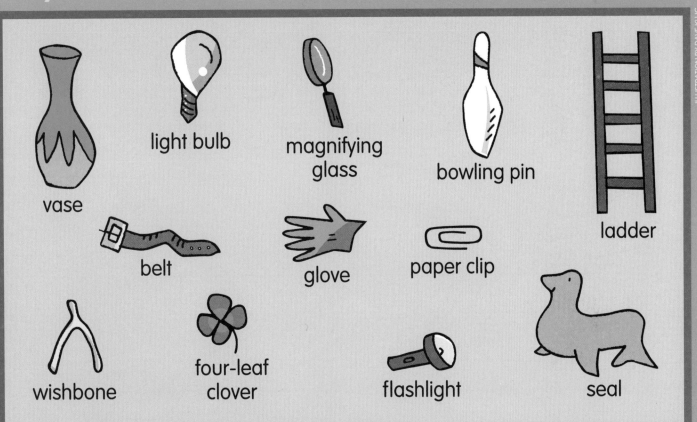

vase

light bulb

magnifying glass

bowling pin

ladder

belt

glove

paper clip

wishbone

four-leaf clover

flashlight

seal

ILLUSTRATION BY DAVE KLUG

Who's Flying By?

Connect the dots from 1 to 26 to see another shore bird.

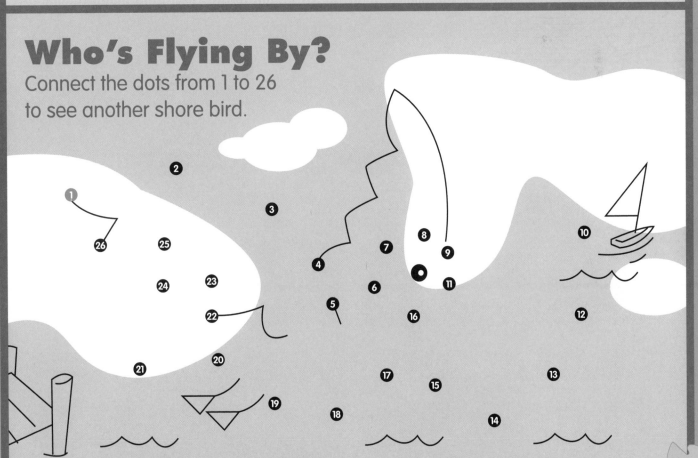

89

Beach Wiggles

These shore things have been knocked sideways in the surf. Can you guess what each one is?

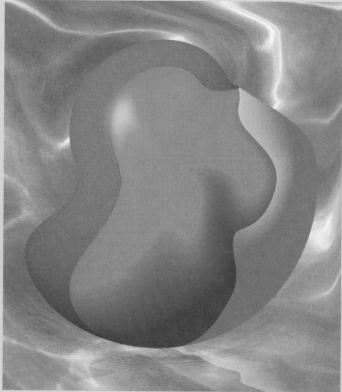

Roving Robots

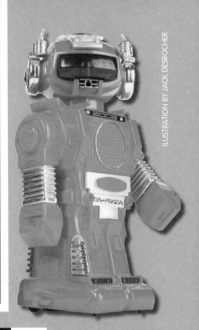

Doodad, Widget, and Whorl have rolled to the corners of this maze. But Glitch is stuck in the middle. Can you help Glitch roll to the empty corner?

Start

Finish

ILLUSTRATION BY JACK DESROCHER

Fish Match

Every tropical fish in the picture has one that looks just like it. Find all 10 matching pairs.

Sports Code

There are four sports jokes on the next page. Use the sports code to fill in the letters and finish the jokes. Then tell them to your friends!

A

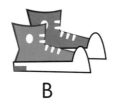

B

C

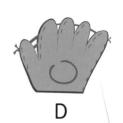

D

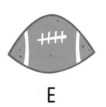

E

F

H

I

L

N

O

R

S

T

U

Y

What did the mitt say to the baseball?

" C A T C H   Y O U

L A T E R . "

What did the two strings do in the race?

T H E   T I E D .

Why did it get hot after the soccer game?

T h e   f a n s   l e f t .

What is a cheerleader's favorite drink?

R O O T   B E E R

Insect Find

The names of 16 insects are hidden in the letters. Some words are across. Others are up and down. We found WASP. Can you find the rest?

Word List

ANT
APHID
BEETLE
BUTTERFLY
CRICKET
DRAGONFLY
FIREFLY
FLEA
GNAT
HONEYBEE
HOUSEFLY
LADYBUG
LOUSE
MOTH
TERMITE
~~WASP~~

```
D R A G O N F L Y X
C M O T H B I Z Q J
R B U T T E R F L Y
I X V Z W E E J T L
C Q G N A T F L E A
K A N T S L L O R D
E V Z J P E Y U M Y
T Z A P H I D S I B
H O N E Y B E E T U
H O U S E F L Y E G
```

96

Dragonfly Duo

Can you find the two dragonflies that are the same?

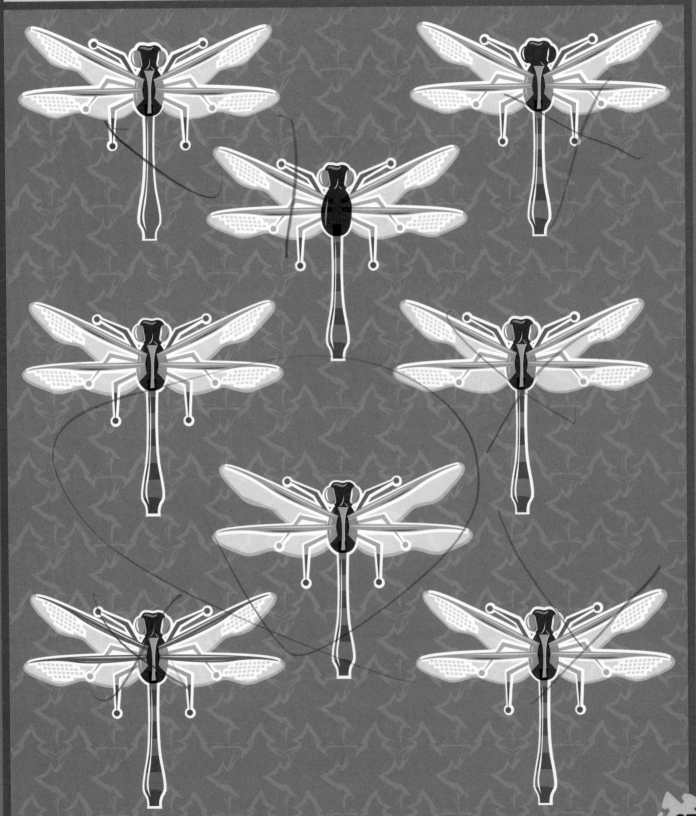

Going Bananas

Zoe, Zippy, and Zak are heading to the playground. Find the path that each will take. Who will pick up the most bananas?

ILLUSTRATION BY DAVID COULSON

FINISH

99

Dog Wash

Can you find these 12 Hidden Pictures® in this soapy scene?

ILLUSTRATION BY DAVE KLUG

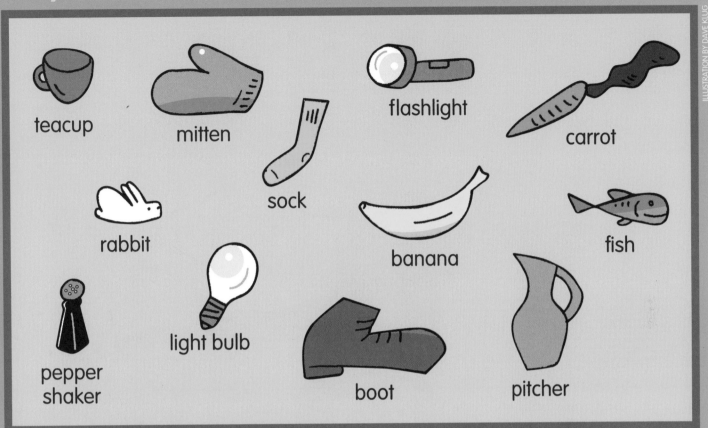

teacup

mitten

sock

flashlight

carrot

rabbit

banana

fish

light bulb

boot

pitcher

pepper shaker

What's for Fido?

Connect the dots from 1 to 30 to see a treat for a dog who has been good.

Seaside Wiggles

These beachside sights have been blown about in the ocean breeze. Can you guess what each one is?

Sports Find

ILLUSTRATION BY JACK DESROCHER

There are 16 sports words hidden in the letters. Some words are across. Others are up and down. We found FOOTBALL. Can you find the rest?

Word List

BASEBALL
BASKETBALL
BAT
~~FOOTBALL~~
GLOVE
GOAL
HOCKEY
HOME RUN
JUMP SHOT
KICK
PENALTY
PUCK
SCORE
SOCCER
TEAM
TOUCHDOWN

```
B A S K E T B A L L
A Z J U M P S H O T
S O C C E R W H X O
E S C O R E X O G U
B A T E A M Z C O C
A P U C K I C K A H
L Q X G L O V E L D
L P E N A L T Y Z O
Q F O O T B A L L W
Z I Z H O M E R U N
```

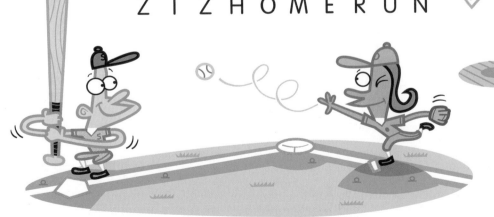

103

Lost and Found

START

Can you help Emma find her lost baseball in this tall grass? Find a clear path from START to FINISH. Happy searching!

FINISH

Double Picnic

It is a perfect day for a picnic! These two pictures are the same but different. What's missing on this page?

Book Nook

What do astronauts like to read? Find the answer by following the line from each letter. Write the letter in that blank space.

In a Word

Each pair of words below is hiding a shorter but related pair. For example, the first pair hides **MOM** and **DAD**. Can you find the other pairs?

1. **mom**ent, doo**dad**
2. struck, cargo
3. badger, goodbye
4. diving, shout
5. charm, bubblegum
6. history, sherbet
7. clover, thunder
8. sunken, honeymoon
9. grunt, boardwalk
10. rocket, stroll
11. frightened, leftovers
12. shower, constellation

Juice Search

Great Skates

Can you find these 12 Hidden Pictures® at the skate park?

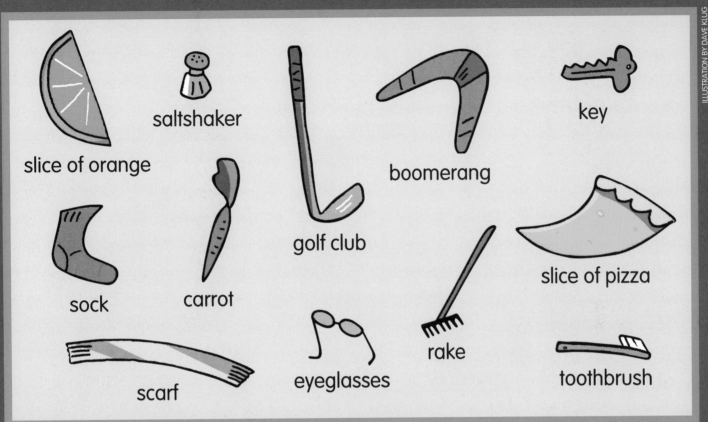

slice of orange

saltshaker

golf club

boomerang

key

sock

carrot

rake

slice of pizza

scarf

eyeglasses

toothbrush

What's on Wheels?

Connect the dots from 1 to 45 to see another fun ride.

Furry Wiggles

These baby animals have been twisted and turned.
Can you figure out what each one is?

Travel Five

1. Which state is bigger—Texas or New York?

2. In what direction does a compass needle point?

3. Circle the cloud that looks like an animal.

4. Name three things you might see in a science museum.

5. Name two purple things you might see at a farmstand.

ILLUSTRATION BY KELLY KENNEDY

115

Lunch Match

Every sandwich in the picture has one that looks just like it. Find all 9 matching pairs.

ILLUSTRATION BY DAVE JOLY

117

Car Code

There are four jokes about cars on the next page. Use the car code to fill in the letters and finish the jokes. Then tell them to your friends!

What kind of cars do toads drive?

_____ _____ _____   _____ _____ _____ _____

What kind of cars do dogs drive?

H o u n d a s

What do police drive at the shore?

S q u i d   C a r s

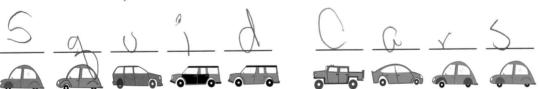

What kind of car do you drive in the fall?

A n   A U T U M N -

M o b i l e

ILLUSTRATION BY MIKE MORAN

Bird Find

The names of 17 birds are hidden in the letters. Some names are across. Others are up and down. We found PELICAN. Can you find the rest?

Word List

OWL
DOVE
GULL
HAWK
IBIS
SWAN
CRANE
EAGLE
HERON
STORK
FALCON
PARROT
PIGEON
PUFFIN
~~PELICAN~~
PENGUIN
FLAMINGO

```
P E N G U I N X Z
U P I G E O N Z X
F E Z E A G L E J
F L A M I N G O J
I I B I S H A W K
N C R A N E X Y G
Q A P A R R O T U
Q N J S T O R K L
F A L C O N O W L
S W A N X D O V E
```

ILLUSTRATION BY JACK DESROCHER

Rocket Launch

121

Perfect Waves

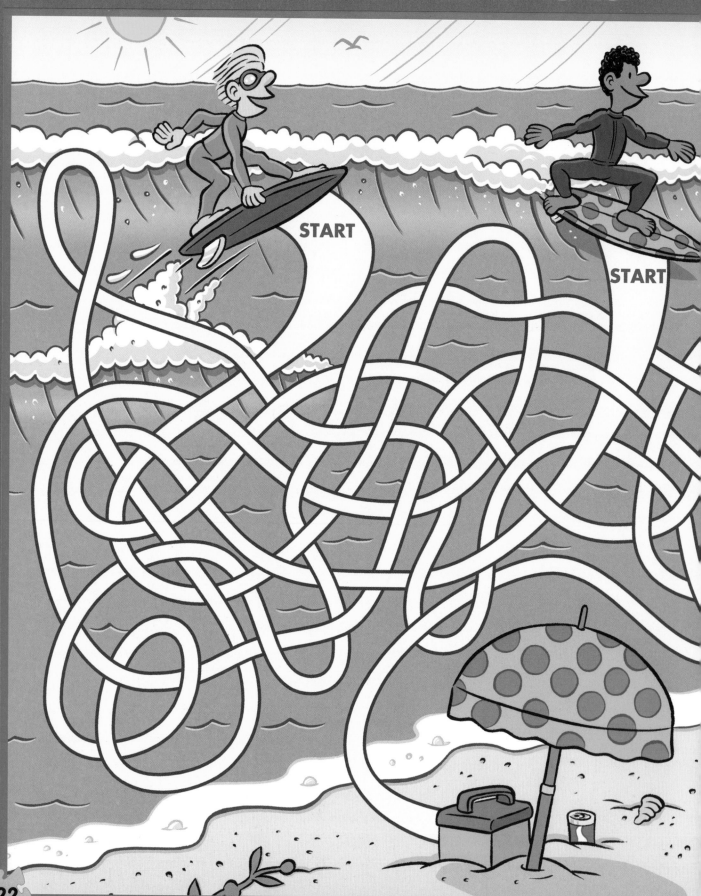

Luke, Logan, and Sandy are zooming to shore. Follow the paths to see where each surfer will dry off.

START

SPF 30

123

C Is For ?

Can you find a clock, a camera, and a couch? What other things can you find that begin with C?

Tongue Twister

Try to say this three times as fast as you can:

Can you can a can as a canner can can a can?

125

Wiggle Play

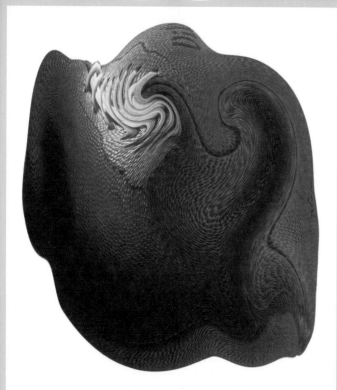

This play equipment is every which way. Can you figure out what each item is?

Land and Sea

ILLUSTRATION BY RON ZALME

Fill-in Fun Color each space that has a dot to see a desert animal.

Color by Number Use markers or crayons to color this fish tank.

Butterfly Away

START

Can you help this butterfly find its way to its friends? Find a path from START to FINISH that is not blocked by anything.

FINISH

129

ILLUSTRATION BY RON ZALME

Critter Count

Soccer Find

There are 18 soccer words hidden in the letters. Some words are across. Others are up and down. We found FOUL. Can you find the rest?

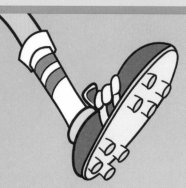

Word List

BALL
CLEATS
DEFENSE
DRIBBLE
FIELD
~~FOUL~~
GOALIE
HEADER
KICK
LOB
NET
OFFENSE
PERIOD
PASS
SAVE
SCORE
SHOT
SIDELINE

C L E A T S M P Q F
W L Z Y Y I D E J I
X O H E A D E R P E
M B A L L E F I A L
D R I B B L E O S D
K I C K Y I N D S S
Q O F F E N S E X H
M S C O R E E Z J O
X J Q U W Z Y N E T
G O A L I E S A V E

Goldfish School

Can you find the two fish that are the same?

Pizza Search

Sal's Restaurant makes the best pizza in town!
Can you find all 21 slices?

ILLUSTRATION BY JANNIE HO

PIZZA

Can you find?

- 1 bib
- 2 pairs of eyeglasses
- 3 drinking straws
- 4 forks

135

Lighthouse Tour

ILLUSTRATION BY DAVE KLUG

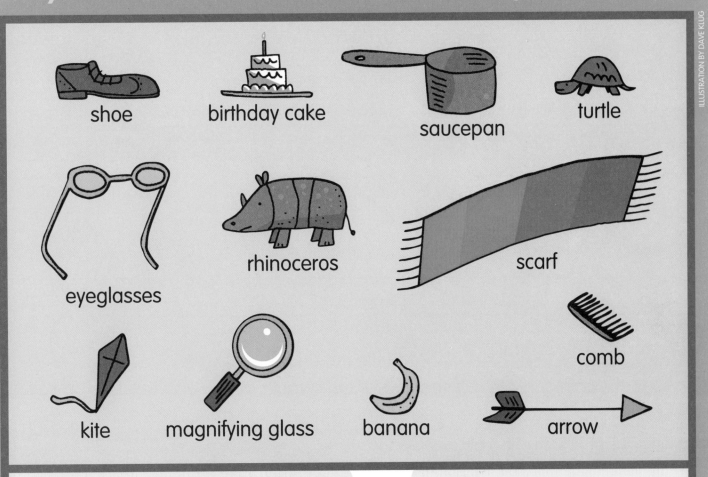

shoe

birthday cake

saucepan

turtle

eyeglasses

rhinoceros

scarf

comb

kite

magnifying glass

banana

arrow

Who's at the Pier?

Connect the dots from 1 to 22 to see someone who likes lighthouses.

137

Animal Five

1. How do you know when a dog is happy?

2. A baby kangaroo is called a joey.
○ True   ○ False

3. Circle the animal that is NOT an insect.

4. Which bird cannot fly?
○ ostrich   ○ flamingo   ○ owl

5. The word "gato" is Spanish for which animal?
○ dog   ○ cat   ○ bird

PET SHOP

ILLUSTRATION BY KELLY KENNEDY

All Talk

We've hidden **20** ways to say something in this grid. They are hiding up, down, across, backward, and diagonally. How many can you find?

Word List

~~BABBLE~~	PRATTLE
BELLOW	PROCLAIM
BLATHER	RAMBLE
CRY	SCREAM
EXCLAIM	SCREECH
HISS	SHRIEK
HOLLER	SPEAK
JABBER	WHISPER
MUMBLE	WHOOP
MURMUR	YELL

S P E A K E T R E E I C
Z M U M B L E L L Y W S
S H H E D T X B B E O H
G Y H X W T B V M L L H
P R O C L A I M A L L H
H S L L B R S H R I E K
C C L A P R M W W B B
E R E I B L A T H E R M
E E R M S H H O I C N C
R A M Q H Z O F S O R D
C M W I Q P V O P I S Y
S E S M J A B B E R H G
M S R U M R U M R E H D

PUZZLE BY CHARLOTTE GUNNUFSON

ILLUSTRATION BY SCOTT ANGLE

Kite Match

Every kite in the picture has one that looks just like it. Find all 10 matching pairs.

Flower Code

There are four flower jokes on the next page. Use the flower code to fill in the letters and finish the jokes. Then tell them to your friends!

A

B

D

E

F

G

H

I

L

M

N

O

P

R

S

T

U

W

What plant loves math?

A _ S _ U _ M _ - _ F _ L _ O _ W _ E _ R

What flower does everyone have?

T _ U _ L _ I _ P _ S

What did the big flower say to the little flower?

" H _ I _ , _ B _ U _ D _ . "

What does a baker like to grow?

A _ F _ L _ O _ U _ R

G _ A _ R _ D _ E _ N

Wiggle Pets

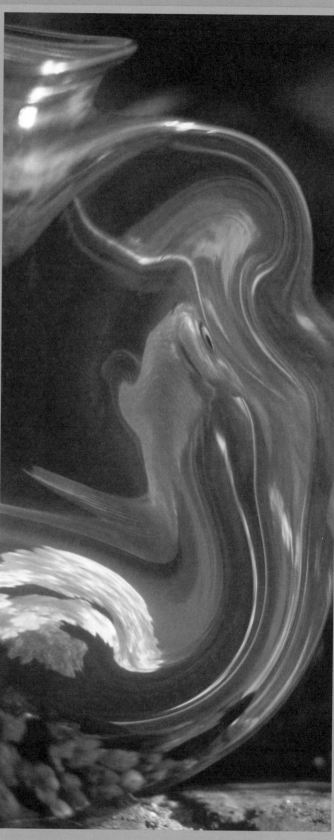

These pets are all in a tizzy. Can you guess what each one is?

Where will each of these skydivers land? Follow the paths to see four safe landings.

START

START

147

Double Dive

Dive on in! These pictures are the same but different. Can you point out what's missing this page?

ILLUSTRATION BY MIKE DAMMER

149

Circle Find

The names of 16 round things are hidden in the letters. Some names are across. Others are up and down. We found DOUGHNUT. Can you find the rest?

Word List

BAGEL
BASEBALL
BUBBLE
CIRCLE
COOKIE
~~DOUGHNUT~~
GLOBE
MARBLE
MOON
ORANGE
PLATE
RING
SNOWBALL
SUN
TARGET
WHEEL

```
F D O U G H N U T F
Y B U B B L E J A Q
B X Y A O Z F R C
A S U N S R I N G O
G L O B E A P X E O
E J Q V B N L W T K
L O O N A G A H M I
M A R B L E T E O E
C I R C L E E E O X
S N O W B A L L N Z
```

Bulldog Bunch

Can you find the two bulldogs that are the same?

Bike Lane

START

Help Kenzie earn her bicycle badge. Find a path from START to FINISH. Do not go past anything blocking your way.

153

Beetle Match

Every beetle in the picture has one that looks just like it. Find all 10 matching pairs.

Sports Wiggles

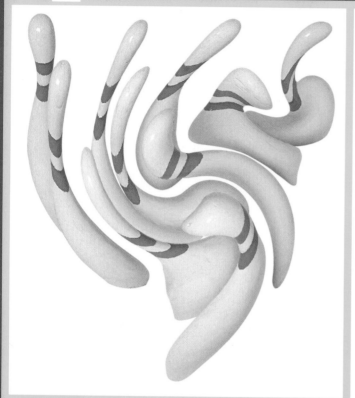

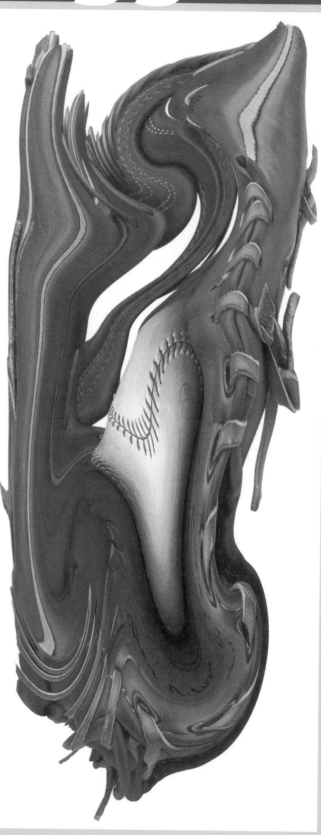

This sports equipment is in a twist. Can you guess what each item is?

Name That Pet

What did Cleo name her new pet snake? To find out, circle the names from the list. (Look up, down, across, backward, and diagonally.) Then write the leftover letters in order from left to right and top to bottom.

Name List

~~CRUSHER~~
DIAMOND
FANG
HISSY
JAKE
KING TUT
MEDUSA
MISS HISS
MONTY
NEFERTITI
NOODLES
PRETZEL
SLIMY
SLINKY
SLITHERS
SNEAKY
TWISTER
WIGGLES

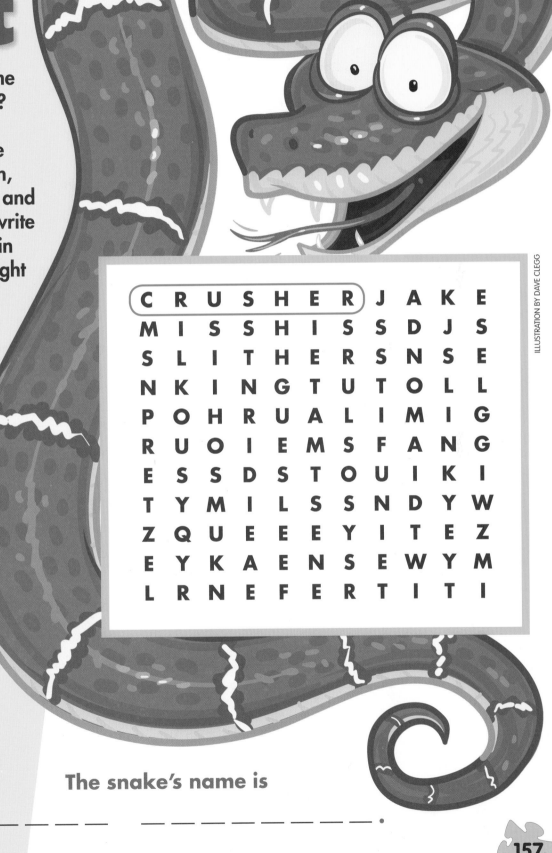

```
C R U S H E R  J A K E
M I S S H I S S D J S
S L I T H E R S N S E
N K I N G T U T O L L
P O H R U A L I M I G
R U O I E M S F A N G
E S S D S T O U I K I
T Y M I L S S N D Y W
Z Q U E E E Y I T E Z
E Y K A E N S E W Y M
L R N E F E R T I T I
```

ILLUSTRATION BY DAVE CLEGG

The snake's name is

_ _ _ _ _ _ _   _ _ _ _ _ _ _ _.

157

Hockey Search

There are lots of hockey sticks at the pond today. Can you find all 15?

Can you find?

- 1 squirrel
- 2 scarves
- 3 hockey pucks
- 4 stars

Camping Out

Can you find the 12 Hidden Pictures® in this camping scene?

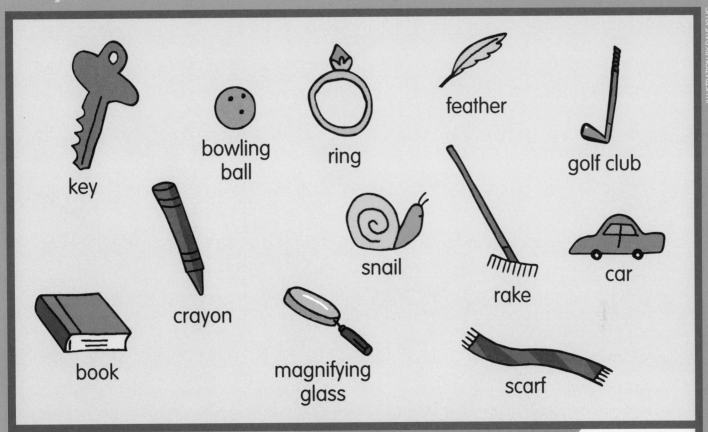

key

bowling ball

ring

feather

golf club

crayon

snail

rake

car

book

magnifying glass

scarf

Who's There?

Connect the dots from 1 to 30 to see a useful camping item.

161

Ocean Find

The names of 16 ocean animals are hidden in the letters. Some names are across. Others are up and down. We found DOLPHIN. Can you find the rest?

Word List

CLAM
CRAB
DOLPHIN
JELLYFISH
LOBSTER
OCTOPUS
SEA HORSE
SEAL
SHARK
SQUID
STARFISH
STINGRAY
SWORDFISH
TURTLE
WALRUS
WHALE

```
S E A H O R S E C J
W A L R U S E A L E
O C T O P U S X A L
R L X S Q U I D M L
D O L P H I N X V Y
F B Z W H A L E X F
I S T I N G R A Y I
S T A R F I S H V S
H E X S H A R K Z H
C R A B T U R T L E
```

Fire Drill

Can you find the two fire trucks that are the same?

ILLUSTRATION BY CLAY CANTRELL

163

Cereal Match

ILLUSTRATION BY DAVE JOLY

Space Code

There are jokes about space on the next page. Use the space code to fill in the letters and finish the jokes. Then tell them to your friends!

A

B

C

D

E

F

G

H

I

K

L

M

N

O

R

S

T

U

W

One of a Kind

Twenty words that contain the letters ONE are hidden in the letters. Look for them up, down, across, backward, and diagonally. There's just one catch. For each word, the letters ONE have been replaced by the number 1. For example, BALONEY appears as BAL1Y. If you can find every one, you're number one in our book!

Word List

- ~~BALoneY~~
- BARITone
- CALZone
- COBBLESTone
- COLoneL
- CYCLone
- DOGGone
- GEMSTone
- LoneLY
- MARIoneTTE
- MICROPHone
- MoneY
- oneSELF
- OPPoneNT
- OZone
- SAXOPHone
- STATIoneRY
- TROMBone
- WISHBone
- XYLOPHone

```
W I S H B 1
M G E M S T 1
1 H P O X A S E
Y P L 1 L Y 1 S L
B A R I T 1 T T E
  X O R S A V
  Y P C E T E
  L P Y L I N
  O 1 C B 1 1
  P N L B R S
  H T 1 O Y E
  1 O D C C L
  T W E 1 S F
  N E T Z G E
  D B A L 1 Y
  O P N A S C
P Q A G M I C R O P H 1
S B X G T R O M B 1 O W
E T T 1 I R A M P O Z 1
```

169

Go-Cart Track

START

START

START

3rd

2nd

Who will win the race? Follow the paths to see who finishes first, second, and third.

1st

By the Tide Pool

Can you find these 12 Hidden Pictures® in this tide-pool scene?

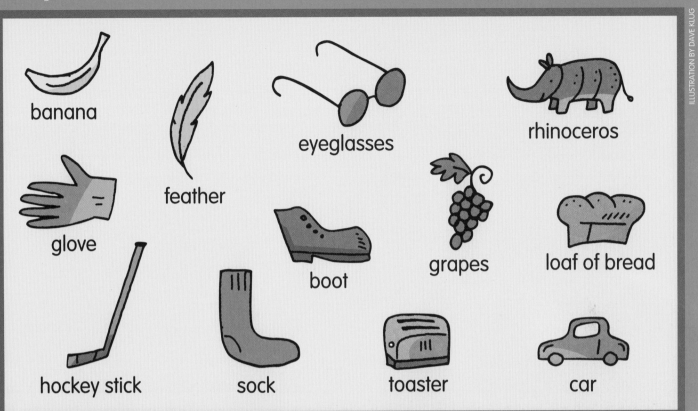

banana

feather

eyeglasses

rhinoceros

glove

boot

grapes

loaf of bread

hockey stick

sock

toaster

car

Who's in the Pool?

Connect the dots from 1 to 36 to see something you might find in a tide pool.

173

Wiggle Swim

These sea creatures have gotten all turned around. Can you guess what each one is?

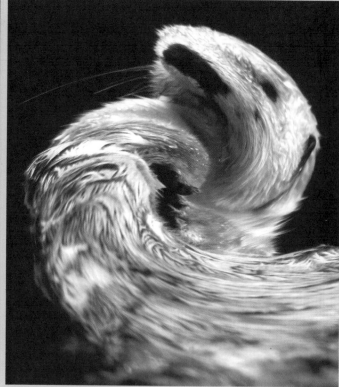

Catch This!

It's a fly ball! Will it be caught or go over the fence? Follow its path to find out!

175

Car Search

Bird Code

There are jokes about birds on the next page. Use the bird code to fill in the letters and finish the jokes. Then tell them to your friends!

A

C

E

F

K

L

M

N

O

P

R

T

U

W

Y

What do sick birds need?

____ ____ ____ ____ ____ ____ ____ ____ ____

What was the goose arrested for?

What's orange and sounds like a parrot?

____ ____ ____ ____ ____ ____ ____

What do you call a wacky chicken?

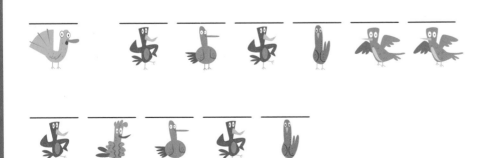

179

Football Find

There are 18 football words hidden in the letters. Some words are across. Others are up and down. We found PUNT. Can you find the rest?

Word List

BLOCK
CENTER
DEFENSE
END ZONE
FIELD GOAL
FUMBLE
HUDDLE
KICKOFF
LINE
OFFENSE
OFFSIDE
PASS
~~PUNT~~
QUARTERBACK
RUN
SACK
TACKLE
TOUCHDOWN

```
J Q V C E N T E R Y
F U M B L E A X U O
I A L I N E C T N F
E R Y K I C K O F F
L T O V J X L U Y F
D E F E N S E C J N
G R F (P U N T) H V S
O B S A H U D D L E
A A I S X B L O C K
L C D S A C K W Y V
X K E N D Z O N E J
```

180

Just Weight!

Emma weighs 78 pounds. She needs to take three one-pound bowling pins across a bridge that can hold only 80 pounds. How can she do it?

To see the answer, follow each line from a letter to a blank space. Write the letter in that space.

ILLUSTRATION BY MIKE MORAN

Sock Match

Every snazzy sock in the picture has one that looks just like it. Find all 10 matching pairs.

Dog Days

START

START

START

START

Each of these dogs has a treat waiting for it. Who will get which one? Start at a dog and follow the path to find out.

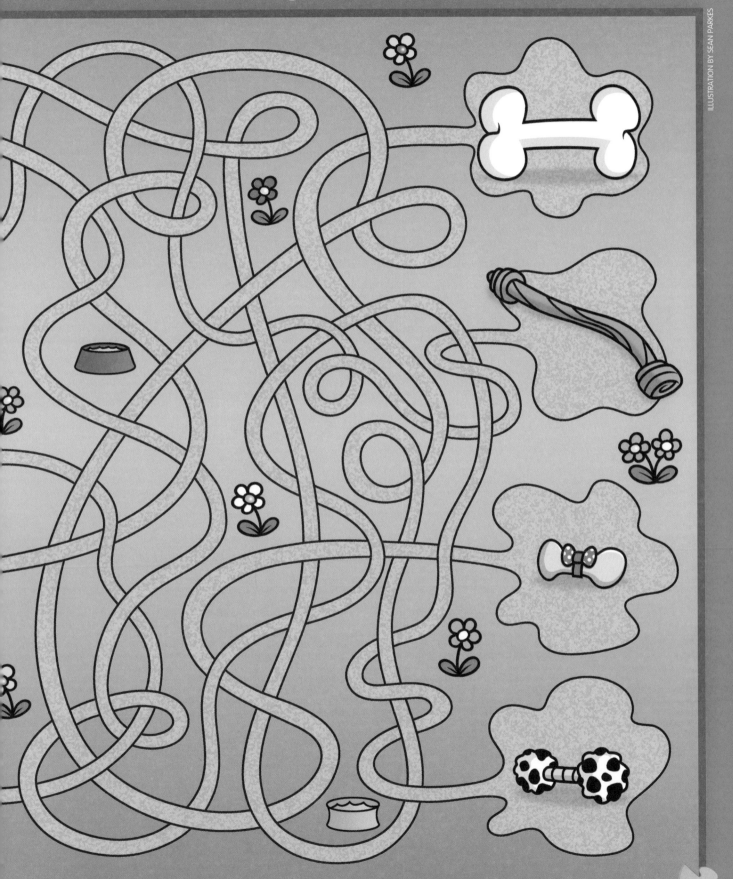

185

Winged Wiggles

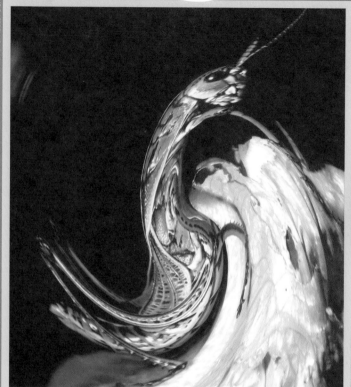

These winged things have gotten all turned around.
Can you guess what each one is?

WORM SEARCH

Twenty kinds of worms are hiding up, down, across, backward, and diagonally in this grid. We circled FIELD. Can you unearth the rest?

Word List

- ~~FIELD~~
- FIRE
- FLAT
- FLUKE
- GLOW
- HEART
- HOOK
- INCH
- MEAL
- NIGHTCRAWLER
- RED WIGGLER
- ROUND
- SEA
- SILK
- SPAGHETTI
- TAPE
- THREAD
- TUBE
- WAX
- WHIP

```
N I G H T C R A W L E R
S P A G H E T T I S D M
P X A W I N C H P R A R
F L U K E M H O O K E E
I R P E D R E C G Y R D
E Z V W N O A Q P I H W
I R Z S U W R Y M W T I
V I I L O K T H O E D G
X L C F R O W L V M A G
K T A P E O G F L A T L
D L E I F B U N B E S E
J E S T U B E P Q X Q R
```

BONUS PUZZLE

The smartest worm of all is hiding somewhere in the grid. Dig deep to find it!

Kitty Playtime

Can you find these 12 Hidden Pictures® in this kitten scene?

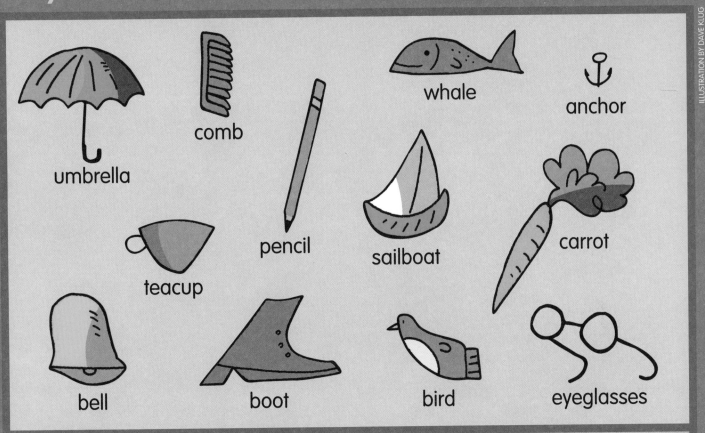

whale

anchor

comb

umbrella

pencil

sailboat

carrot

teacup

bell

boot

bird

eyeglasses

ILLUSTRATION BY DAVE KLUG

What's That Cat?

Connect the dots from 1 to 41 to see a very different kind of cat.

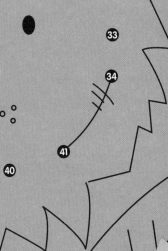

Treasure Hunt

START

190

Can you help Pete find the pirate treasure? Follow the path from START to FINISH without bumping into anything.

FINISH

Car Find

There are 16 car words hidden in the letters. Some words are across. Others are up and down. We found **HEADLIGHT**. Can you find the rest?

ILLUSTRATION BY JACK DESROCHER

Word List

CAR
HOOD
HORN
TIRE
DRIVE
TRUNK
WHEEL
AIR BAG
BRAKES
BUMPER
ENGINE
GASOLINE
SEAT BELT
DASHBOARD
~~HEADLIGHT~~
WINDSHIELD

```
W H E E L C A R H G
I O X T R U N K O A
N O Q B U M P E R S
D D R I V E F J N O
S E A T B E L T Z L
H E A D L I G H T I
I X A I R B A G Q N
E T I R E N G I N E
L Q B R A K E S X Y
D A S H B O A R D Z
```

BLOOMING HUMOR

Count the number of petals on each flower. Then write the matching code letter in the flower's center. Fill in all the flowers to find the answer to the riddle.

KEY

3 - E	9 - K
4 - D	10 - A
5 - I	11 - T
6 - R	12 - B
7 - H	13 - W
8 - G	14 - L

What did the dog do after he swallowed a firefly?

Lizard Search

LIZARDS

Can you find?

Can you also find five prairie dogs in the picture?

ILLUSTRATION BY DONNA CATANESE

Cat Code

There are four cat jokes on the next page. Use the cat code to fill in the letters and finish the jokes. Then tell them to your friends!

What does a cat call its grandfather?

G R A N D - P A W

What kind of kitties like to go bowling?

A L L E Y C A T S

What's a cat's favorite color?

P U R R - P L E

What do cats say to each other in the morning?

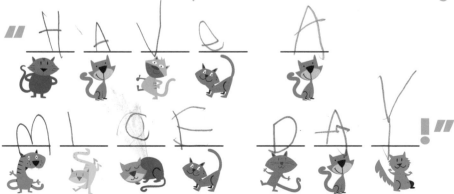

" H A V E A

M I C E D A Y !"

Wiggle Rides

These outdoor rides has been twisted and turned.
Can you guess what each one is?

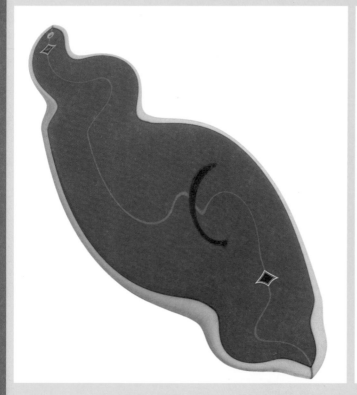

Night Flyers

Fill-in Fun Color each space that has a dot to see a night flyer.

Color Copy Use markers or crayons to make a UFO that matches.

199

Beach Match

Every shell in the picture has one that looks just like it. Find all 10 matching pairs.

ILLUSTRATION BY DAVE JOLY

201

Meerkat Mix-Up

START

START

202

These four furry meerkats need a rest. Follow the tunnels to see where each one belongs.

START

START

203

Veggie Find

The names of 18 vegetables are hidden in the letters. Some words are across. Others are up and down. We found LETTUCE. Can you find the rest?

Word List

BEANS
BEET
CABBAGE
CARROT
CELERY
CORN
CUCUMBER
EGGPLANT
KALE
~~LETTUCE~~
MUSHROOM
ONION
PEAS
PEPPER
POTATO
RADISH
SPINACH
SQUASH

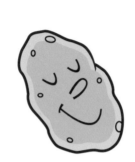

```
C A B B A G E Z W B
E G G P L A N T C E
L V P O T A T O U A
E K O N I O N B C N
R A D I S H F E U S
Y L E T T U C E M Q
P E P P E R C T B U
M U S H R O O M E A
C A R R O T R X R S
P E A S P I N A C H
```

Dino Dash

ILLUSTRATION BY DAVE CLEGG

Mega Mort loves his in-line skates. To learn more, fill in each of the spaces below. Use each word just one time, and they have to rhyme!

Word List

by	last	roar
eye	places	soar
fast	prize	~~sport~~
flies	races	

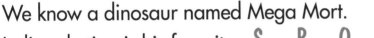

We know a dinosaur named Mega Mort.

In-line skating is his favorite <u>S P O R T</u>.

He goes to many ___ ___ ___ ___ ___ ___ ,

To enter lots of ___ ___ ___ ___ ___ .

He skates on ___ ___ ,

In the blink of an ___ ___ ___ .

He goes so ___ ___ ___ ___ ,

He never comes in ___ ___ ___ ___ !

Mort just ___ ___ ___ ___ ___ ,

Always winning first ___ ___ ___ ___ ___ .

Hear the crowd ___ ___ ___ ___

When they see that dino ___ ___ ___ ___ !

Family Reunion

ILLUSTRATION BY DAVE KLUG

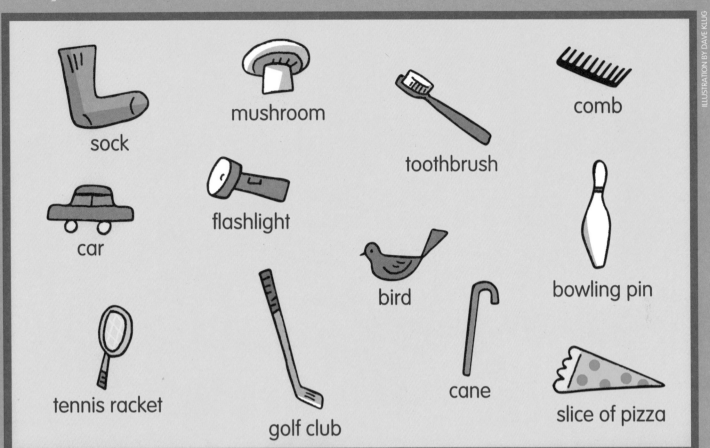

sock

mushroom

toothbrush

comb

car

flashlight

bird

bowling pin

tennis racket

golf club

cane

slice of pizza

What's Cooking?

Connect the dots from 1 to 26 to see a picnic sizzler.

Fin-ish Line

START

Can you help the little fish swim back to its friends? Find a safe path from START to FINISH. Watch out for sharks!

FINISH

ILLUSTRATION BY RON ZALME

Zoo Wiggles

These animals' names all start with the letter P.
Can you guess what each one is?

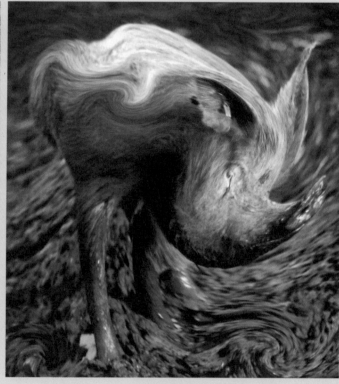

Say Cheese!

We've hidden 22 kinds of cheese in the grid. Look for them up, down, across, backward, and diagonally.

Word List

AMERICAN
ASIAGO
BLUE
BRIE
CHEDDAR
COLBY
COTTAGE
EDAM
FETA
GOAT
GORGONZOLA

GOUDA
LIMBURGER
MONTEREY JACK
MOZZARELLA
MUENSTER
PANEER
PARMESAN
PROVOLONE
RICOTTA
ROQUEFORT
SWISS

Bonus! Can you sniff out another word that goes well with cheese?

```
Q R I C O T T A G E V B D R
M H S W I S S S O S G N G H A
L O M I B F A Y B I O O A D
W S N R A T E F O U A R M D
Y X I T V X Y L D R A G M E
B E V U E P I A J E N O O H
L I M B U R G E R E A N Z C
O E P A R M E S A N M Z Z M
C N B R E A D Y X A E O A A
O N F C D E D R J P R L R C
T R O F E U Q O R A I A E A
P R O V O L O N E R C X L R
W M A D E B I F V F A K L O
C N C R A C K E R S N V A N
S M U E N S T E R E I G L I
```

211

Food Code

There are three food jokes on the next page. Use the food code to fill in the letters and finish the jokes. Then tell them to your friends!

A

B

C

E

F

G

H

I

K

L

M

N

O

P

R

S

T

U

W

Y

212

What did the mustard say during the race?

"

       "

Why did the cookie see a doctor?

       -   .

How do you fix a broken pizza?

213

S Is For ?

Can you find a skunk, a scarecrow, and a statue? What other things can you find that begin with the letter S?

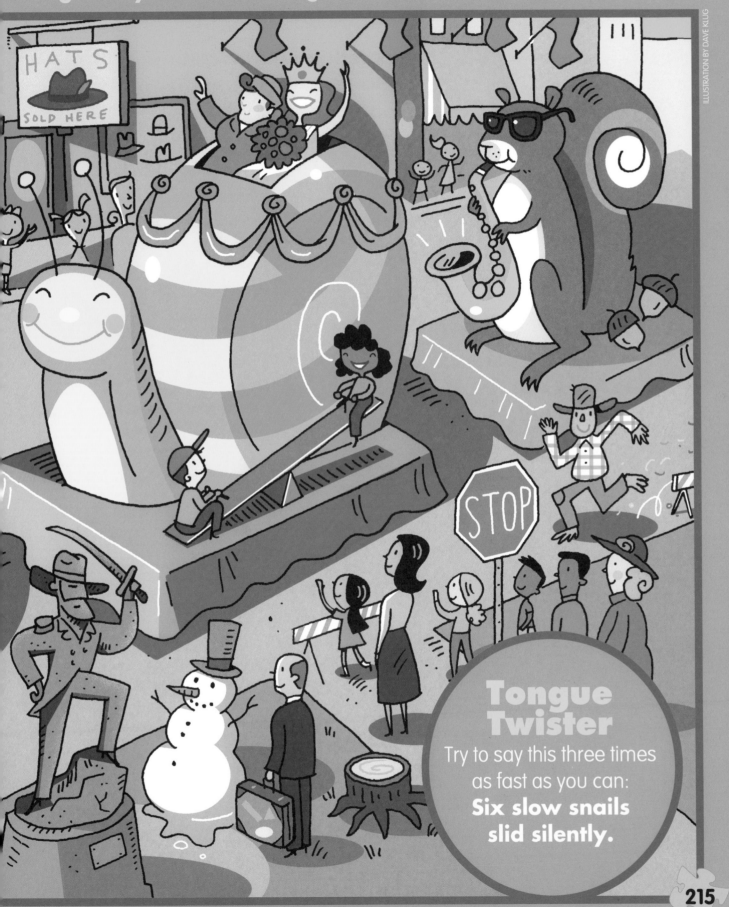

ILLUSTRATION BY DAVE KLUG

Tongue Twister

Try to say this three times as fast as you can: **Six slow snails slid silently.**

215

Robot Rows

Each of these robots has something in common with the other two robots in the same row. For example, in the first row across all three robots are on wheels. Look at the other rows across, down, and diagonally. Can you tell what's alike in each row?

216

Answers

5. Galaxy Quest

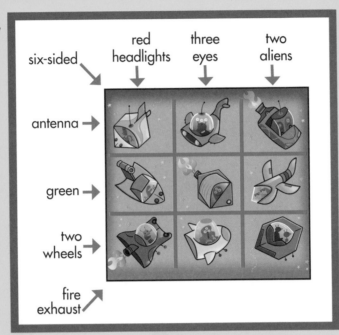

six-sided → red headlights three eyes two aliens

antenna →

green →

two wheels →

fire exhaust →

6. Beach Find

```
K O C E A N B A L L
X J K S H E L L F H
J Q S E A G U L L A
J Y X S W I M S U I T
T O W E L S H S A P B
R Y A C J U O V P R
E Q V H X N V N F E
E S E A W E E D L E
Y P A I L X L K O Z
S T A R F I S H S E
```

7. Shell Game

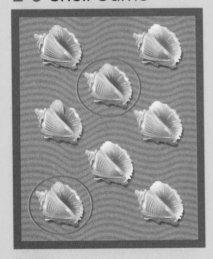

8. Rhino Route

10. Double Pets

12. Wiggle Snacks

sandwich

grapes   loaf of bread

13. Play It

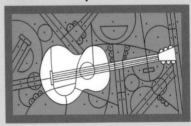

It's a guitar!

217

Answers

14. Caps Search

16. At the Movies

17. What's Playing?

18. Critter Five

1. Rug, bug, and mug
   Did you think of others?
2. Reindeer, moose, and rhinoceros
3. Circle the leopard on the left.
4. True
5. China

19. Treat Trail

20. Balloon Match

Answers

22. Frog Code

Q. What is a frog's favorite drink?
A. Croak-a-cola

Q. What did the bus driver say to the frog?
A. "Hop on!"

Q. Where do frogs make notes?
A. On lily pads

Q. What do frogs wear on their feet?
A. Open-toad shoes

24. Boat Find

25. Parrot Pals

26. Funny Flights

28. S Is For ?

Here are the **S** words we found.
You may have found others.

1. sun	11. spoon	21. soccer ball
2. star	12. spider	22. saltshaker
3. sand	13. shovel	23. sunglasses
4. slide	14. sailboat	24. sand castle
5. shark	15. sea horse	25. scuba diver
6. sheep	16. spaghetti	26. screwdriver
7. scarf	17. seashells	27. shopping cart
8. stairs	18. shamrock	28. sun hat
9. stove	19. surfboard	29. smile
10. swing	20. snowflakes	30. splash

30. Wiggle Insects

ladybug

caterpillar

butterfly

31. Color It

It's a whale!

Answers

32. Touchdown!

34. Double Desert

36. Name Five

1. She is playing a trombone.
2. True
3. Cindy, Catharine, and Carmen
   Did you think of other names?
4. Fish, turtle, lobster, whale
5. Jupiter

37. Pie Way

38. Bow Search

40. In the Kitchen

41. What's for Dinner?

Answers

42. Tree Find

```
J A S P E N O W Q
V F P A L M A K X
B I R C H Y K L R
E R U Z J P I N E
E Y C E D A R U D
C H E S T N U T W
H Q L V P E A R O
X Z M A P L E Y O
Y J D O G W O O D
W I L L O W A S H
```

43. Caterpillar Pair

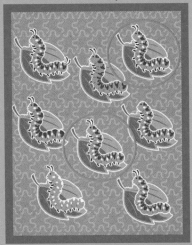

44. Flag Match

46. Dinosaur Code

Q. What do you call a sleeping dinosaur?
A. A stego-snore-us

Q. What do you call a worried dinosaur?
A. Nervous rex

Q. What does a triceratops sit on?
A. Its tricera-bottom

48. Wiggle Wheels

train

motorcycle   school bus

49. Ride It

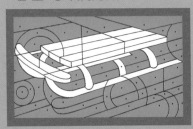

It's a sled!

Answers

50. Cat Course

52. Count On It!

54. Lunch Find

```
C T A C O C H I P S
R V W E T U R K E Y
A P P L E J U I C E
C B R E A D M I L K
K A G R A P E S W P
E N X Y O G U R T E
R A I S I N S Z V A
S N C O O K I E E C
W A T U N A F I S H
S O U P C H E E S E
```

55. Swim Twins

56. Roll With It!

58. Double Serve

222

Answers

60. Field Wiggles

mouse

frog

snail

61. Wing It

It's an eagle!

62. Ball Search

64. Zoo Stars

65. Who's at the Zoo?

66. Travel Find

```
M O T O R C Y C L E
D C A N O E S H I P
F J X Z W A G O N L
S A I L B O A T Z A
U S C O O T E R D N
B I K E A V D A K E
W Q J D T A F C A R
A T R A I N Q T Y Z
Y F J T U G B O A T
Z D T R U C K R K Q
```

67. Moon Landing

223

Answers

68. Bunny Match

70. Fruit Code

Q. What do you call an apple that plays the trumpet?
A. Tooty fruity

Q. What is a ghost's favorite fruit?
A. Boo-berries

Q. What do you call a cat that eats lemons?
A. A sour puss

Q. What are two banana peels on the floor?
A. One pair of slippers

72. Wiggle Gear

kayak and paddle

swim gear   tennis racket

73. Wild Things

It's an elephant!

74. Leash Twist

76. A Is For ?

Here are the **A** words we found.
You may have found others.

1. apple
2. ape
3. arrow
4. alien
5. armor
6. acorn
7. ax
8. artist
9. ace
10. antenna
11. address
12. anteater
13. animals
14. actor
15. antlers
16. airplane
17. archer
18. anchor
19. alligator
20. addition
21. acrobat
22. alarm clock
23. automobile
24. aquarium
25. accordian
26. audience

Answers

78. Soccer Find

```
C L E A T S M P Q F
W L Z Y Y I D E J I
X O H E A D E R P E
M B A L L E F I A L
D R I B B L E O S D
K I C K Y I N D S S
Q O F F E N S E X H
M S C O R E E Z J O
X J Q U W Z Y N E T
G O A L I E S A V E
```

79. Bug Buddies

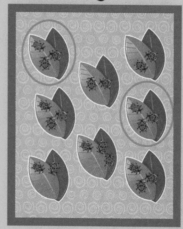

80. In the Deep

82. Double Builders

84. Wiggle Babies

foal

chick

bear cub

85. Nothing to It!

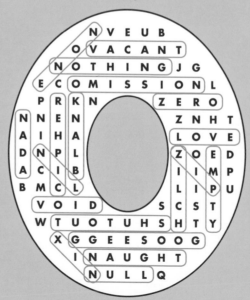

225

Answers

86. Flag Search

88. Bird Watchers

89. Who's Flying By?

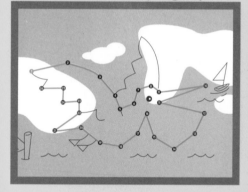

90. Beach Wiggles

starfish

sand pail   beach ball

91. Roving Robots

92. Fish Match

94. Sports Code

What did the mitt say to the baseball?
"Catch you later."

What did the two strings do in the race?
They tied.

Why did it get hot after the soccer game?
The fans left.

What is a cheerleader's favorite drink?
Root beer

Answers

96. Insect Find

```
D R A G O N F L Y X
C M O T H B I Z Q J
R B U T T E R F L Y
I X V Z W E E J T L
C Q G N A T F L E A
K A N T S L O R D Y
E V Z J P E Y U M B
T Z A P H I D S I U
H O N E Y B E E T G
H O U S E F L Y E G
```

97. Dragonfly Duo

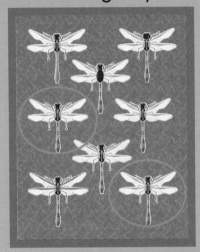

98. Going Bananas

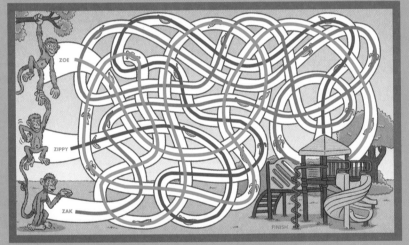

Zoe picks up 10 bananas, and Zippy and Zak get 8 each.

100. Dog Wash

101. What's for Fido?

102. Seaside Wiggles

sea gull

seashell   palm tree

103. Sports Find

```
B A S K E T B A L L
A Z J U M P S H O T
S O C C E R W H X T
E S C O R E X O G O
B A T E A M Z C A U
A P U C K I C K L C
L Q X G L O V E L H
L P E N A L T Y Z D
Q F O O T B A L L O
Z I Z H O M E R U N
```

Answers

104. Lost and Found

106. Double Picnic

108. Book Nook

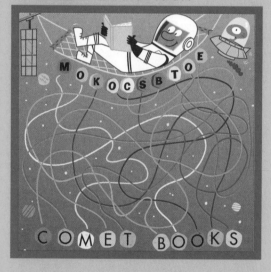

109. In a Word

1. mom, dad
2. truck, car
3. bad, good
4. in, out
5. arm, leg
6. his, her
7. over, under
8. sun, moon
9. run, walk
10. rock, roll
11. right, left
12. show, tell

110. Juice Search

Answers

112. Great Skates

113. What's on Wheels?

114. Furry Wiggles

polar bear cubs

calf

puma cubs

115. Travel Five

1. Texas is bigger.
2. North
3. Circle the cloud in the middle.
4. A dinosaur skeleton, a robot, and an aquarium
5. Plums and eggplants

Did you think of others?

116. Lunch Match

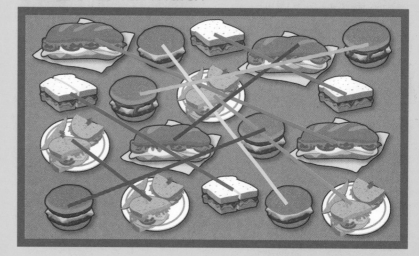

118. Car Code

Q. What kind of cars do toads drive?
A. **Hop rods**

Q. What kind of cars do dogs drive?
A. **Houndas**

Q. What do police drive at the shore?
A. **Squid cars**

Q. What kind of car do you drive in the fall?
A. **An autumn-mobile**

120. Bird Find

P	E	N	G	U	I	N	X	Z
U	P	I	G	E	O	N	Z	X
F	E	Z	E	A	G	L	E	J
F	L	A	M	I	N	G	O	J
I	I	B	I	S	H	A	W	K
N	C	R	A	N	E	X	Y	G
Q	A	P	A	R	R	O	T	U
Q	N	J	S	T	O	R	K	L
F	A	L	C	O	N	O	W	L
S	W	A	N	X	D	O	V	E

121. Rocket Launch

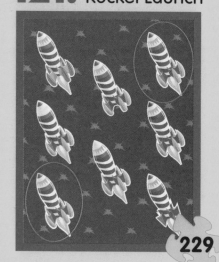

229

Answers

122. Perfect Waves

124. C Is For ?

Here are the C words we found.
You may have found others.

1. cat	12. crown	23. cowboy
2. cattails	13. coin	24. candle
3. car	14. crib	25. castle
4. cow	15. crane	26. compass
5. cup	16. cap	27. crab
6. cane	17. carrots	28. cracker
7. cub	18. cactus	29. camel
8. cake	19. camper	30. clown
9. coat	20. crayons	31. cricket
10. corn	21. canoe	32. caterpillar
11. cage	22. cookie	33. calculator

126. Wiggle Play

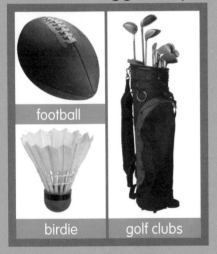

football

birdie

golf clubs

127. Land and Sea

It's a camel!

128. Butterfly Away

130. Critter Count